The children in Rob's class got to
come to Family Day.

Rob's father, mother, and Gram
did a lot!
They got on the Big Dot Team.

Rob got the Big Dot flag.
Rob did not drop it.

Rob and his Gram jumped in the
frog hop.
The big black clock said they had
won.

4

Rob's mom ran on Big Rock
Track.
His mom ran on top of ten big
fat logs!

Lots of people got hot, hot, hot.
They ran, ran, ran to the dock.

Rob jumped in the pond. Plop! Plop!
Rob's dad did a big flip flop.

Here is a picture of the glad Big
Dot team.
Your family will love Family Day,
too!